GRIEF THAT GRIPS THE HEART

By Yashica Allen Lee

Published by Hadassah's Crown, LLC

Laurens, SC 29360

Copyright © 2018

All rights reserved. No part of this book may be reproduced, scanned, or distributed in any printed or electronic form or by any means without prior written consent of the publisher, except for brief quotes used in reviews.

Please do not participate in or encourage piracy of copyrighted materials in violation of the author's rights. Purchase only authorized editions.

Library of Congress Control Number: 2018940011

Grief That Grips The Heart

ISBN 978-0998123059

Printed in the United States of America

Dedication

**This book is in memory of my mom.
Her unconditional love will always be remembered.**

Acknowledgements

Thank you to my family and my support team who prayed and encouraged me during this difficult time. I appreciate you all more than you will ever know.

My grandson, Korbin, you are an amazing little boy who has certainly brought me great joy at the perfect time.

My husband, Tracy, thank you for always believing in me and pushing me to face all my fears.

My publisher, Hadassah's Crown Publishing, founded and operated by Dr. Sonia Cunningham Leverette, thank you for your guidance and your willingness to help me get through this process.

Contents

Foreword	7
My Personal Experience	11
Grief Defined	14
Preparing for the Arrival	17
The Arrival	19
The News	25
Healing	30
Overcome	35
Stages	39
NEVER Say To Someone...	43
Scriptures to Meditate On...	46
About the Author	50

Foreword
By The Family

There are so many things that come to mind about the author of this book. She is a true woman of God, wife, mother and grandmother. In life, we go through tests, but there is no greater test than losing a loved one you are close to. This was one of the most difficult tests the author has experienced. I saw firsthand how grief gripped her heart. I was also privileged to see how she could overcome the grip of grief.

I thank God that when she was at her lowest point, she trusted Him to get her through this time. When she realized she was not alone, it made dealing with grief easier. It was a long process, but our support team was committed to walking through this process together. I believe every reader will be blessed by this book and will be able to share how they were able to overcome the grip of grief.

Husband, Tracy

Have you ever had someone in your life who lights up your world? The unique sound of their laughter or their encouraging words always seem to make things better. This person is your best friend, the one you can call any time of day and chat for hours, have lunch or dinner dates with faithfully or spend numerous hours shopping. These things describe the bond the author had with her mother. Imagine your world being crushed by the sudden death of your mother and best friend. The pain of losing a loved one is one of the most difficult things one might experience. The author pours her innermost thoughts and emotions out in this read. She gives the stages of grief and shares how she overcame the bondage of grief. She is an inspiration and has helped her family members overcome grief as well. It is my hope that the author's transparency will help others overcome.

Daughter, Zalika

The author of this book is an inspiration to many. She is a woman of God, a mother and a mentor. While overcoming grief, she became a stronger woman mentally, emotionally and physically. Writing this book allowed her to be transparent with her struggles. She gives others hope to overcome a difficult situation in life. Her openness and words will inspire others daily.

Son, Tra

Grief is something that can't be weighed nor timed, but it's something that we all can truly say one day we will all have to endure, cope with and ultimately overcome. I shared the pain of watching the author grieve, as well as her joy that allowed her to continue to stand strong and diligent with her faith in God. In this book, you will understand how to utilize your faith in God to overcome not just grief, but any obstacle that may be in your life. Enjoy this book in all its sincerity, but also remember to love, pray and most importantly, understand that God will not put more on you than you can bear.

Son, Devin

My Personal Experience

The excitement of having Spring Break had finally approached. No vacation was planned for the family, just a simple week of resting, studying and being home. We always looked forward to spending this week at one of our favorite vacation spots. This was very much out of the ordinary for our family not to travel during Spring Break.

It was a nice spring morning, April 2, 2015. I sat on my bed studying and preparing for a seven-sermon message I was scheduled to deliver in two days. As I turned my laptop computer off, my cell phone began to ring. Looking at the unfamiliar number, I immediately processed in my mind I would not answer the call. Just as I made the decision I heard a calm faint voice direct me to answer. The caller on the other end asked, "Are you Julianna?"

I did not recognize the caller's voice, so my response was "Who's speaking?"

The caller proceeded by making me aware my mom had become very ill at a local restaurant. For a short time, I had to process what I heard from the caller. Speechless for a moment, I knew I had to get there quickly.

"Okay ma'am, which restaurant? I will be there shortly."

Her response was, "NO, you need to go to the hospital."

She informed me she had performed CPR, my mom was unconscious and Emergency Medical

Services had placed her in the ambulance. This was the beginning of a very, very long journey of grief that gripped my heart.

Grief Defined

What is grief? Grief is a deep sorrow that is caused by death, separation, heartbreak or dejection. It often becomes overpowering and the emotions tend to be overwhelming. Grief is a natural response our bodies go through when we lose someone or something that held a special place in our lives. Grief will grip the heart at the very core.

When grief grips the heart, it can consume every area of life. The heart may feel it has been shattered into many pieces with no hope of being repaired. The Bible speaks of how Jesus wept with the family of His close friend, Lazarus, in John 11:35. This is a perfect illustration of how grief does not discriminate.

There are no two people who will experience grief in the same capacity, so different people's grief experiences should not be compared. The mind and body process things differently and at a different velocity. One may internalize grief while the other may handle it externally. However, internal grief can be detrimental to the body when the pain is harbored on the inside. There is nothing wrong with grieving when it is done in a healthy manner. When an individual grieves in an external manner, they find an outlet that allows them to release the emotions. Positive outlets will include solely trusting God, seeking grief counseling, a close friend or family member who will listen even if you repeat the same information multiple times. I dare not suggest everyone will need a professional counselor. Consequently, if there is not a person to confide in, I do suggest you seek a professional counselor. Their position is to assist in managing grief and providing coping skills to assist with the different emotions.

Being totally honest during sessions is critical. I was blessed to have a strong support team I could always count on when I needed to talk or a shoulder to cry on. I shared stories that would lighten the sadness I was experiencing. With no shame in admitting I was in a terrible place, I had to seek a professional who helped me manage the grief that gripped my heart. Persons grieving should find that safe place that allows them to deal with the pain of grief.

Preparing for the Arrival

As I prepared myself to leave home for the hospital, deep in my gut I knew I was going to walk into a situation that would not look promising to my natural mind. Along the way, other than saying, "LORD HELP," I could not find the strength to pray a prayer I felt would reach Heaven quickly. I called my husband, my brother and my close friend to request they begin to bombard Heaven on my mom's behalf. My travel was not that far, but when it is an emergency, five minutes feel like two hours.

Approaching the hospital, I began to feel knots in my stomach because I did not know what was before me. What was I about to face? This was not how the Thursday of Spring Break was supposed to be. The last conversation I shared with my mom was the two of us being together on this day but certainly not in a hospital setting. No day is promised. Enjoy every moment; cherish absolutely every moment with those you love. Celebrate every moment like it will be your last encounter.

The Arrival

"Excuse me, ma'am. I'm Julianna and I received a call my mom was being transported here by Emergency Medical Services. Will you check to see if she has arrived? Her name is Delores Clemons."

"Yes, she is, but I cannot allow you to go back at this time."

Can you imagine the look on my face and the pain I felt at that moment? Pacing back and forth, I could only think of what could possibly be going on that was keeping me from being in there.

After about fifteen minutes, my nerves would not allow me to leave the receptionist alone.

"Excuse me, Ma'am. I need to speak with someone immediately about my mom's condition."

Before she could respond, I began to ask her a series of questions. So nervous, I did not give her time to answer before I was asking another question. Panicking, I continued to say I need to know what is going on.

"Can you tell me if my mom is still breathing?" As pleasant as she could be, she informed me someone would be out shortly to assist me.

I watched the door continuously until it opened and the voice of the Patient Advocate said "Family of Ms. Clemons, you can come in the family room. The doctor will be in shortly."

Grief gripped my inner being because I knew things could not be good if the family room was where I was headed. My question again... "Is my mom still breathing?" Please tell me before the doctor comes in. The response was, "Yes, but the doctor will need to explain the severity of your mom's condition."

Impatiently waiting, I will never forget the words I heard from the doctor.

"Your mom is very sick. We have her on a life support machine. Her situation is critical. Her vitals are not good. She is not responding at this time. We plan to do additional tests. She will be transported upstairs to our critical care unit and monitored closely. Are you the person we need to contact as we provide for her medical care? Give us a few minutes and we will let you go back to see her."

I thought I was ready but I was indeed not ready for the words I heard. I could feel the tears as they welled up in my eyes. My mom had been a strong woman and had overcome many medical obstacles in the past. But what was different about my faith in her pulling through this time? This time was different than the times we experienced before. My heart desperately wanted her to pull through but for some reason I could not get my faith to line up. I struggled to apply, "Faith is the substance of things hoped for and the evidence of things not seen." I knew God and felt I had a strong relationship with Him, but I needed my faith to line up so He could perform the miracle I so desired.

Stepping into the glass door that was covered by a long curtain, I could see my mom looked nothing like herself. She was lying on a bed hooked to multiple machines and she was unaware of her surroundings. I had no clue what to say or do, so I gently placed my hand on her hand and assured her I would not leave her side. I knew I had absolutely no control over the outcome.

All I wanted was for God to perform a supernatural miracle. The miracle I desired was for Him to heal her completely so she could be here with me. To be quite honest, I was being completely selfish because I did not want my mom to be out of my presence. I thought she was too young to die and I was too young to be without her. I never considered the fact that God could answer my request if it meant she had to be with Him.

Deuteronomy 31:6 says, "Be strong and courageous. Do not be afraid or terrified because of them, for the LORD your God goes with you; He will never leave you nor forsake you."

I did not feel strong nor courageous. I was afraid of what the next moment would hold. During this moment, I felt my strength and courage had vanished so quickly. It seemed the odds were against what my eyes could see.

The News

Deep in my heart, I felt my mom's condition had improved slightly. I continued to pray and hoped things were better than they appeared. Easter Sunday approached rapidly as I waited for the doctor to give me a detailed prognosis. Several days had passed with a trail of tests and multiple visits from medical specialists and nurses. Surely after four days I was about to hear a small sound of hope from the voice of a doctor. The appointment with the doctor was scheduled for the afternoon of Easter. After meeting with the doctor, I believe my heart shattered even the more after hearing these words.

"We have done all we can do. Julianna, you need to make the

decision to take your mom off life support."

Oh, how painful, how excruciating, how agonizing the feeling my heart was experiencing. I felt as though my very own life had been snatched from me. I wanted this cup to pass from me because I could not bear this pain on my own. This was the moment my heart was gripped by grief that took me to a whole new level. I knew there would not be another opportunity for me to text, call my mom by phone, shop with her, feast on another Sunday meal at her home, travel together, hear sound advice, laugh until my stomach hurt at the hilarious comments she made or to hear those precious words "I LOVE YOU" multiple times a day. Certainly, this doctor did not expect me to make such a vital decision on today?

My heart was gripped by the pain and from the things I would miss so dearly. The grip of grief does not begin once your loved one takes their last breath. Grief can begin as soon as the communication is no longer a two-way dialogue. When there is no longer a verbal dialog or no other way to communicate, grief can begin its course.

"Blessed are those who mourn for they shall be comforted." (Matthew 5:4)

You can find comfort in knowing God is with you every step of the way, even when it feels you are alone. Grief that grips your heart will make you feel isolated with no hope of ever being released from the pain.

It is stressful to watch a loved one struggle through their last days of life, even if you know there is eternal life after this journey.

After seven days of life support, I made the decision to let life take its course. Why?? Because I knew this was not my mom's ideal quality of life. By no means was this an easy task. It was unfair to allow her to struggle to live when God was already preparing for her to live in eternity with Him. She was an independent woman who loved and lived life to the fullest. She enjoyed life and always strived for others to enjoy it as well. I could no longer prolong her freedom by allowing her life to be stagnated by a machine.

The life support machine was disconnected on Thursday at noon. God's will was completed in thirty-eight hours. He chose to add another precious jewel to His eternal home. I knew my mom was whole again, but I was devastated and I desperately needed God to come see about me.

Healing

Will the tears ever go away? In time, they dry up somewhat. Those moments of crying are good because they are a part of the cleansing and healing process; they release emotions and mitigate stress. I cried when people knew I was crying; I cried when people had no idea I was crying. I would often smell something that reminded me of my mom and I would cry. The tears came at unexpected times. Believe me, I did my share of crying.

There was a time I could not talk about my mom without becoming emotional. Just to reflect on the unconditional love she gave unselfishly to others would cause me to cry.

"Weeping may endure for a night but joy comes in the morning." (Psalms 30:5)

Night may seem as though it is a long trail of ups and downs. Continue to hold on until your morning comes. Morning does not come because you have forgotten about the one who has been temporarily removed. It comes because God has given you the ability to cope with the emptiness until you reunite again.

Grieving is a process that is often denied for the fear of being judged by others. It is a necessary journey you must deal with after the loss of someone who played a major role in your life. You must grieve in a healthy manner in order to heal in a healthy manner. Every person heals differently. Healing begins when you accept the fact you are not in control of life.

For twenty-two months, I was in a terrible place of grief. I didn't know how I would make it from day to day. I knew how to fake a smile; I knew the dialogue to use so others did not know the pain I was feeling. My heart was broken into numerous pieces, but I had to trust that God was able to mend every broken piece. I needed time to heal and time to learn to live life again.

For almost two years, I was not in a place to minister. No matter the title, we are human. Life will sometimes hurt ministers to the core. Many of us have been programmed to believe that we must operate in our brokenness. Some would say, "You have a call on your life and you must minister anyway." God has called us to do a work but He need ministers to take care of themselves so they can minister effectively. God does not intend for ministers to be superficial or fake their way through so they appear to be superheroes. He desires for those who minister to be transparent so others can overcome their struggles through our testimonies.

I was unable to minister to myself in the place I was in. I needed God to restore that which was broken. A piece of my heart was broken from the grief I was experiencing. My heart was gripped by grief and during this time, I had nothing to impart to others. I had to trust Him completely during this most difficult time. When I completely trusted Him with all that was in me, I was able to experience my mourning being turned into joyful dancing.

"He (God) will take away the clothes of mourning and cloth us with joy." (Psalm 30:11)

Overcome

In the course of grief, seek healthy ways to get through the grieving process. Unhealthy grieving can lead to sin and choices that are not beneficial. Sin will not remove your pain. In fact, it will eventually magnify your pain. I frequently used a journal to document my thoughts for the day. No matter what type of day I experienced, I wrote it down. If I remembered a special time or remembered a time my mother and I laughed with one another, I wrote it down. Write those thoughts down even if you have to cry through it. The journal will allow you to look back years later and see how God helped you through one of your most difficult times.

Spend time worshipping and praying to God. Worship Him no matter how bad the pain may be. Spending time worshipping allows Him to captivate your heart and take you out of the realm that is causing you so much pain. You might not always feel like worshipping, but the ending result is amazing when you have rested in His arms. God is still good and He deserves your continuous worship.

Set aside time to pray to God. Ask Him to help you get through this painful time. Prayer is the time you spend sharing the depth of your heart and soul with God. There is absolutely nothing you cannot talk to God about. He desires a one-on-one conversation with you. Share your brokenness with Him. You do not have to articulate every word correctly nor have a long drawn out speech for Him to hear you. A short prayer is fine. He knows your heart and He will be right there to console you. Just spend some one-on-one time in His presence. Through your prayer time, God begins to minister to your broken heart and begins to release the grip of grief.

Though you have lost someone that held a special place in your heart, you can continue to celebrate the life they lived. Take a walk down memory lane and relive those special times you shared with them. What made the person happy? What made the person shine? You must continue their legacy. Determine what made them light up. Use it to pay tribute to them and allow it to be a part of the process that helps you overcome grief. Do something to continue the legacy they began. They were special to you, so it is up to you to celebrate them through stories, pictures, foundations, scholarships, annual donations, or adopting a responsibility they participated in. You may choose to create a flower garden or a memorial space in honor of your loved one. The most important idea is to continue to celebrate the life they lived.

Stages

There are many stages of grief. You may experience a stage more than once and it is possible not to experience one of the stages. One stage may be short-term, while another may take what feels like eternity to overcome. The stages include the following:

-Shock/Numbness

- Guilt/Anger

-Helplessness/Reasoning

-Depression/Loneliness

- Feeling of Wanting to Die

-Acknowledgement

I experienced every one of these stages and probably a few more were added to the list. Each stage was different and was handled differently. Cope with grief one day at a time. It is neither healthy nor wise to place a timeframe on the process. One day might be great but the next day might not be as easy. Deal with the day as it comes. Do not get discouraged because your life does not spontaneously return to normal. There is no quick-fix to the healing process. There is a time and season for all things to heal. One day, you will smile again; one day you will experience joy again. Today may not be the day but keep pressing through until that great day comes.

Depression was the stage that lasted the longest for me. I was depressed to the point I did not feel like my mind was capable of processing anything. I did want to work, did not want to go to church and did not want to live. My bed and my closet were the places I would run to when I entered my home. These were the places I thought brought me comfort. Depression is real and it will change your entire outlook on life. Your mental capacity becomes altered from its normal functioning ability. It causes your mind to be consumed with many different thoughts. The thoughts may not always be the thoughts you desire to have. The enemy will use your mind as a playground if you allow him to.

Do not allow yourself to stay in that dark place. The longer you stay there the harder it is to get free. I know that if it had not been for God, things could have been different for me. It was the grace of God that rescued me and my strong inner circle who continuously prayed for me. The scripture I used most was Psalm 3:3.

"Lord, you are a shield around me and you lift my head high." Psalm 3:3

I knew I did not want to take medication to temporarily coat my battle with depression. After dealing with depression for way too long, I wanted to be healed completely. Therefore, I had no choice but to trust that God would truly be the one to lift my head from the place I was in.

If you cannot shake depression, seek medical attention. There is absolutely nothing wrong with taking medication if you have no other option. All of our stories will not be the same.

NEVER say to someone who is grieving:

I know how you feel. (You will never fully know how someone else feels.)

He/She lived a long life. (No life is too long when you really love someone.)

You had them for many years. (So what? The number of years does not fill the void.)

You should be over that by now. (There is no timetable for grief.)

You will get over it. (You learn to cope with the separation.)

It does not take all that. (Every experience is unique.)

You are a Pastor/Minister so you do not need counseling. (God is the greatest counselor. However, professional counselors are trained to do a job for those who have titles.)

The most helpful thing to do for someone who is grieving is to provide a listening ear. Often, silence or a hug is the best help that can be provided. Your thoughts should simply be your silent thoughts. Spoken thoughts could cause someone to experience a deeper level of grief. Choose your spoken words wisely. Seek to build and not obliterate.

You must accept you have no control over when your loved ones leave this earth. As much as you would like to have them present, the day will come when they must go to the place where they can rest eternally. Your hope is in knowing if you accept Jesus Christ as your personal Savior, Heaven will one day be your home. The experience of grief allows you to know through the difficult times in life, God is still with you. It may seem at times He remains quiet and is not there. Be encouraged. He remains by your side through it all.

Grieve healthily and grieve completely so you can become whole again. Physical bodies will leave us. When they do, we can cling to wonderful memories that will last a lifetime. We are victorious; we are more than conquerors. With God, we can get through grief that grips our hearts.

Scriptures (New International Version) to mediate on when grief grips our hearts:

Psalm 18:2	The Lord is my rock, my fortress and my deliverer; my God is my rock, in whom I take refuge, my shield and the horn of my salvation, my stronghold.
Psalm 34: 18	The Lord is close to the brokenhearted and saves those who are crushed in spirit.
Psalm 46:1-2	God is our refuge and

strength, an ever-present help in trouble.

Lamentations 3:31-33   For no one is cast off by the Lord forever. Though He brings grief, He will show compassion, so great is His unfailing love. For He does not willingly bring affliction or grief to anyone.

Matthew 5:4   Blessed are those who mourn, for they will be comforted.

Matthew 11:28	Come to me, all who you who are weary and burdened and I will give you rest.
John 14:1-4	Do not let your heart be troubled. You believe in God; believe also in me. My Father's house has many rooms. If that were not so, I would have told you that I am going there to prepare a place for you. And if I go to prepare a place for you,

I will come back and take you to be with me that you also may be where I am. You know the way to the place where I am going.

Revelation 21:4

He will wipe every tear from their eyes. There will be no more death or mourning or crying or pain, for the old order of things has passed away.

About the Author

Yashica Allen Lee is a native of Anderson, South Carolina, where she resides with her husband, Tracy. They have a daughter, Zalika, and a son, Tra. Minister Lee completed her Bachelor's Degree in Human Resources and Masters in Christian Ministry, both at Anderson University. Minister Lee was ordained in 2014 and has a desire to share God's Word in a way that is understandable to all. She strongly believes when we encounter trials, we must press through those times so we can see God's glory manifest in the end.

Author Contact Info: yashical@yahoo.com
or facebook.com/yashica.lee

About the Publisher

Interested in publishing or for more information about Hadassah's Crown Publishing or other publications by the company, visit www.HadassahsCrownPublishing.com, email soncunnlev@gmail.com or call 864-708-1214.

www.ingramcontent.com/pod-product-compliance
Lightning Source LLC
Chambersburg PA
CBHW050448010526
44118CB00013B/1742